TASTE
LONDON

ISSUE 1 · SEP. OCT. 2022 · THEREADERSHOUSE.CO.UK

- Media & Restaurant Business
- GOOD FOOD & GREAT VIBES, Efes, London's Finest Cuisine since 1974
- Taste joy after every sip, Could sherbet be the new drink of the UK?
- Kunefe POWER, Sofra makes its way

Glorious
City & Taste

INTERV
GO
Azure In
SUSA
Aut
of

ED
W

available at

Dive

Into a Great Journey

Ready to
share
your
story?

The Reader's House
Make a phenomenal start
thereadershouse.co.uk

Enrich Your Life

World's Classics

100 Greatest Novels of All Time

www.iboo.com

IN THIS ISSUE

Here's the glorious city & taste

Lots to see, do and eat in London, If you're visiting or living. Just keep in mind what to see and do in London before we talk about its food and Top restaurants, cafes, cuisines and bars.

On the cover of this we feature London's best and cozy restaurants, categorized by countries and subjects. These selected best and cozy restaurants yet of course they are not the only one. You think as a restaurant owner and manager, or a customer we missed yours, please contact us editor@thereadershouse.co.uk One of our editors will contact and visit you.

SCAN TO READ EMAG

EDITOR'S LETTER

Welcome to First issue of Taste London magazine that connects restaurants, cafes, bars, food and beverage businesses that share their story and passion. We bring them long-form writings on different topics and unique interview, review and news subjects.

On the cover of this we feature London's best and cozy restaurants, categorized by countries and subjects. These selected best and cozy restaurants yet of course they are not the only one. You think as a restaurant owner and manager, or a customer we missed yours, please contact us editor@thereadershouse. co.uk One of our editors will contact and visit you.

Following weeks and months we'll release more anymore localized magazines including Coventry, Cambridge, Oxford, Birmingham, Manchester and even other cities like New York, Los Angeles, Paris, Roma, Vienna and so on.

London Taste and other localized magazines are more than magazine. It is available in electronic, flip and in print, over 190 countries and more than 40.000 online stores, retailers and libraries. It is available forever, and you can get it electronic or print from selected online stores including Amazon, Barnes & Noble, Waterstones, Blackwell's...

In this issue; on page 18, Fatih Oncu wrote Media and Restaurant Business, explains how media contributes your restaurant business action. It is a prescription of restaurant and any other businesses.

"Do These 5 Important Steps Before You Start Grilling" on page 22, Adrian T. Cheng tells you what to do for a tasty grilled meat.

"Fast Food and Calories" on page 26, Karen Sessions wrote how does fast food negatively affect our daily life.

Full of amazing stories, reviews, advice and news, you'll have so much fun with our new issue of Taste London of this issue.

Enjoy reading...

Published by
Newyox Limited
200 Suite
134-146 Curtain Road
EC2A 3AR London
t: +44 20 3695 0809
editor@thereadershouse.co.uk

thereadershouse.co.uk

Since the Corona-19 affect in England, we are working remotely until further notice.

Currently, we are still producing publications; should this change, we will contact any customers this affects. This means our phones have been turned off and we're currently only available by email
(editor@entrepreneurprime.co.uk) and whatsapp at +44 79 3847 8420.
We will be answering emails as quickly as possible and we thank you in advance for your patience and understanding. We'll keep our website updated as and when things change.

A. Harlowe
Editor
editor@thereadershouse.co.uk
Dan Peters
Content Editor
dan.peters@thereadershouse.co.uk
CONTRIBUTOS

Bengal Tiger Restaurant

(Cover Image)

Tony A Grayson

F. Oncu

Adrian T. Cheng

Karen Sessions

Tim Halloran

Cumba Gowri

Sridevi Balamurugan

Shahi Masala

Tony A. Grayson

Mickey Mikkelson

Jon Allo

Oladimeji Ajegbile

Rrodnae Productions

Tim Halloran

Here's the glorious city & taste

Lots to see, do and eat in London, If you're visiting or living. Just keep in mind what to see and do in London before we talk about its food and Top restaurants, cafes, cuisines and bars.

London is a great place to eat, drink, chat, meet friends and colleagues or just take it easy. You can pop-in to enjoy a delicious breakfast, filling lunch or a light pre-show meal, drink or snack. London is gothic grandeur. London is vibrant culture. London is pure magic.

LONDON IS PURE MAGIC

One of the world's most visited cities, London has something for everyone: from history and culture to fine food and exceedingly good times. 2000 years of history has made the 'Big Smoke' deeply cosmopolitan and exotic. With such diversity, London's cultural dynamism makes it among the world's most international cities.

WHY AND WHERE TO VISIT

A trip to the capital wouldn't be complete without seeing the top 10 attractions in London. Visit now to enjoy these top things to do in London without the crowds.

From literature to restaurants, history to the Queen, there many reasons why London is one of the greatest cities.

Iconic Buildings

With over 2,000 years of history, there are more iconic buildings and landmarks in London than pretty much any other city in the world. The Shard, St Paul's Cathedral, Tower of London, British Museum, Houses of Parliament., Tate Modern , The Gherkin and London Aquatics Centre are some of them.

Culture

The culture of London concerns the music, museums, festivals and lifestyle. London has frequently been described as a global cultural capital and is one of the world's leading business centres, renowned for its technological

readiness and economic clout, as well as attracting the most foreign investment of any global city. As such, London has often been ranked as the world's capital city.

The Queen

She represents over 1000 years of British tradition, values and democracy.

London is forest

London falls under the UN's definition of a forest. Yes It'is. If you'ere in London, you're in the forest. Gorgeous parks, gardens are dotted all over the city.

Multicultural City

London is the capital city of England, but it is also one of the most multicultural cities in the world. As a matter of fact, one-third of all Londoners are foreign-born, and over

PHOTO BY HUMPHREY MULEBA

200 languages are spoken throughout its many streets and neighbourhoods.

WHERE TO EAT

We are with a long list of amazing places to try, and many of them are new in London. Sure, some things have changed since the pandemic. Business hours are shorter, and finding somewhere to eat on a Monday or any other days of the week can be challenging.

We are Londoners who are wildly passionate about all the delicious food found around this world-famous and historic city. It is true that English food has a bit of a bad reputation, however London Taste changes that view. Our magazine editor's visited some of the restaurants. Once eaten, your mind will chance! London is great city to eat.

BREAKFAST

Granger and Co.

Granger and Co. make their ricotta hotcakes (that's pancakes to you and I) thick and fluffy, with a texture as light as heavenly clouds. They're served with banana and honeycomb butter, giving you just the right amount of sugary sweet energy to start your day.
grangerandco.com

Terry's Café

Terry's Café is family run and the food is all top quality and locally-sourced. The meats they use are from Smithfield Market – where Terry worked before opening the café – and their fresh produce comes from Borough Market. They stick to a traditional breakfast of sausage, egg, bacon, bubble and squeak, black pudding, beans, tomatoes and mushrooms.
terryscafe.co.uk

BUFFET

The Mughal's Indian

There are few things as satisfying as a well done Indian

PHOTO BY CHRIS J MITCHELL

buffet. The buffet takes place daily during lunch time, or all day on Sundays. If you want to eat at the Sunday evening buffet for dinner you will need to make a reservation.
mughalsrestaurant.uk/

Sonargaon

Bringing the tastes and delights of Indian food in Whitechapel.

So whilst you may want to start your meal with a classic pakora starter or a traditional tandoori dish, you also have the option to embrace a bit of English culture and indulge yourself in a Chicken Tikka Omelette.
sonargaonwhitechapel.co.uk

CHICKEN WINGS

JolliBee

Move over KFC, in the Philippines and England it's all Jollibee. Go around and ask Filipinos, and I am sure that this has always been part of their celebrations and milestones. A party is not a party without it!
jollibee.uk

Clutch Chicken, Hoxton

For a more health-conscious dinner, try this intimate, rustic-chic dining room that offers up buckets of free-range chicken fried using healthy oils.
clutchchicken.com

SEA FOOD

Lyon's | Crouch End

With its chipped vintage tiling, Lyon's old-school decor might look modest but it's actually an elaborate ploy to win diners in with low expectations, and then wow them with Penang fish collars and jerk sea bream.
lyons-restaurant.com

The Seafood Bar | Soho

msterdam offshoot The Seafood Bar is a haven for pescatarians – and a challenge to anyone who fancies themselves as having a big appetite.
thenudge.com

KEBAB

Efes

Efes serves to Londoners since 1974 in Mile End, Maple Street and Dartford.
efesrestaurantbar.co.uk

Sofra

One of the London's first Turkish Kebab House founded and managed by legend Chef Huseyin Ozer.
sofra.co.uk

LEBANON CUISINE

JolliBee

Lorem Impsum. Ut rerunt doluptate late cusanitatet landelique non pore vit aceptat.

Eque int, idemollabore nim aborum,
jollibee.uk

JolliBee

Lorem Impsum. Ut rerunt doluptate late cusanitatet landelique non pore vit aceptat.
Eque int, idemollabore nim aborum,
jollibee.uk

INDIAN

Bengal Tiger

Tikka Makes You Holla!
Bengal Tiger is an authentic Indian restaurant and bar, located on the heart of the city; in Old Street
bengal-tiger.co.uk

Silka

A taste of home
Silka Urban Indian resteurant is situated right at the entrance of Borough Market. Silka specializes in delicious Indian Urban cuisine featuring fresh ingredients and masterful preparation by their culinary team.
silka.co.uk

ITALIAN

Figo

Figo reflects both the tradition and the modern aroma of cucina italiana! Each selection of our menu has been carefully selected from specific regions that have evolved

it's taste over centuries of good eating.
figorestaurant.co.uk

Sulu

Sulu promotes healthy eating and drinking that will suit customers from different lifestyles, background and age groups.
mysulu.com

MEXICAN

El Pastór

Inspired by the 1987 cult classic The Lost Boys, this oxymoronically (self five for the excellent word) friendly pizzeria boasts a killer 80s sou.
tacoselpastor.co.uk

Temper

While temper's offering has seen a slight shift since lockdown, their USP remains the same: excellent quality, in-house butchered meat and traditional corn tacos.
temperrestaurant.com

MIDDLE EAST

Layalina & Privée

A restaurant, bar and cabaret club in Knightsbridge, Layalina is one of the best places in London for Middle Eastern food. From the decor to the dishes, this Beauchamp Place beaut looks to highlight the fun and opulence of Lebanese dining with everything from cocktails and canapés, to 7-course spreads.
layalina.co.uk

EartH Hackney

It may look like nothing fancy from the outside, but wait till you step inside EartH Hackney and you'll be taken aback by the stunning interiors of this multi-use space. Check out the bar and kitchen where you'll find stuffed pitas and salads inspired by Tel Aviv.
earthackney.co.uk

PIZZA

Lost Boys Pizza

Lorem Impsum. Ut rerunt doluptate late cusanitatet landelique non pore vit aceptat.
Eque int, idemollabore nim aborum,
lostboyspizza.com

Manifesto

An unassuming spot tucked away in Clapham Junction, Manifesto gambles that sourcing the very best ingredients will result in the very best pizzas.
manifestopizza.com

SPAGHETTI

Padella

If there's currently a London pasta cult, then Padella surely has to be the charismatic leader.
padella.co

Lina Stores

Good things come to those who wait. After 75 years as a smashing Soho deli, Lina Stores decided the time was ripe to try their hand at running a pasta restaurant a few years back.
linastores.co.uk

STEAK HOUSE

Steakout

Originating in early 2008 Steakout tooks the known into the unknown; taking the all so common beef steak, tenderising, marinating with unique flavours and serving in our sizzling Steakout style.
steakoutuk.com

PHOTOS BY MEDIA GATE DIGITAL AGENCY

GOOD FOOD & GREAT VIBES

London's Finest Turkish Cuisine since 1974

"There are tens of Efes restaurants in the United Kingdom. If you don't see the portrait of me on the wall, you're not in the Efes Restaurant" says Mr. Kazim Akkus, estaplished his first restaurant in 1974.

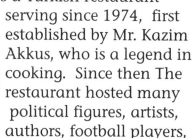

Efes is a Turkish restaurant serving since 1974, first established by Mr. Kazim Akkus, who is a legend in cooking. Since then The restaurant hosted many political figures, artists, authors, football players, and actors, not just from the UK, but all around the globe including Turkey and the States.

> " The dining room is dominated by windows that warms the hearts of local residents. The atmosphere is very good. The lighting is right both for day and evening. And table settings is perfect. People aren't seat on top of each other.

TASTE

Best place if you're looking for a combination of shich, hot chicken, superlative beef satay and a deranged energy that combines excellent food with a Turkish soundtrack constantly on the verge of gabber, this Turkish restaurant is for you.

ATMOSPHERE

Efes atmosphere is very good. The lighting is right both day and evening. And table settings is perfect. People aren't seat on top of each other. They have a good amount of space between them.

PRICE

Starts from £4.95
Kebab £11.99
Mixes Kebab £18.50
Desert £5

LOCATION

230 Mile End Rd,
Stepney Green, London E1 4LJ
020 7790 8890

I've always experienced a delicious main course and caring staff at Efes Turkish Restaurant on Mile End Road, in Stepney Green. I visit there for lunch or dinner and always delighted by the authentic Turkish main course; shish kebab, doner, steak and grilled spicy chicken. Lentil soup to vegitable soup, sea bass to mixed kebab, spices and flavors, baklava to Turkish coffee are extremely impressive for a kebab lovers.

Award winning restaurant Efes is a Turkish cuisine serving since 1974. First established by Mr. Kazim Akkus, who is a legend in cooking for more then 40 years. Since first established, The restaurant hosted many political figures, artists, authors, football players, and actors, not just from the UK, but all around the globe including Turkey and the States. Yet currently Efes is managed by new partner with a mix of contemporary and authentic design on Mile End Road, right across Stepney Green underground, a few stops a way from Liverpool street train station.

We have known Efes Turkish restaurant famous for Kebabs.

This blending of old and new is also seen in the food. The menu features traditional Turkish Kebab fare, but there are some surprises: One of the vegetables offered is stir-fried mixed vegetables, soap, bulgur pilavı and fish of the day and fruit plate and the desserts baklava, sutlac and cheese cake. Another surprise is the restaurant doesn't offer any alcohol drink, and the chicken, beef and all kebabs are all Halal which is particularly associated with Islamic dietary laws and especially meat processed

and prepared in accordance with those requirements.

The dining room is dominated by windows that warms the hearts of local residents. The atmosphere is very warm. The lighting is right both day and evening. And table settings is perfect. There is a table setting outside as well. Inside, people aren't seat on top of each other. Tables have a good amount of space between them. The atmosphere is warming, but happily the food is better than that at most restaurants in the town.

HALAL FOOD
NO ALCOHOL

For those who do not eat meat, the best bet is the lentil and vegetable soups, priced according to the market and size. On the night of my visit it was $24.50 for a two person mixed kebab, combination of all meat and two differens rice and salad. The seabass fish is another nonmeat possibility. It was fresh, good and garnished with grilled fresh onions and green papers.

Mix of mezze is another option before main course that the mezes are cold - probably a wise decision made to take the pressure off the kitchen. If you prefer to begin with something hot, try the soup lentil, a soup with lentils as its main ingredient; it is vegetarian, and is use red lentils without the husk. Dehulled red lentils disintegrate in cooking, making a thick soup. It is a staple food throughout Europe, Anatolia, Latin America and the Middle East.

Overall, I always enjoy my experience in Efes. They did take the time to make the table and meal ready, the main course was good, the staff was caring and the desert especially the sutlac (milk and rice) were perfect.

I'd love to visit again. I'd recommend it as a nice place to go with friends, family or partner. Don't forget the visit Efes on Mile End if you visiting London or living in London

Spooning a Banana

BY
TONY
A GRAYSON

In 2008, during a classroom break, as I sat around a table with a dozen people I met four days earlier, a young lady took a banana out of her purse, peeled it half way, then she took out a spoon and began to carve the peeled banana into spoon-sized bites. She carried on normal conversation while she fed herself spooned pieces of the banana. I had never before seen or heard of anyone who ate a banana that way. My other classmates did not act as if anything about this was unusual. There was another detail that I will reveal at the end of this article.

This is 2021, and something triggered my memory of the event. Now, I can say, thirteen years later, that it still is the only time I have ever seen or heard of anyone who ate a banana that way. You may be familiar with the Jerry Seinfeld television comedy series. Season six featured an episode titled, "The Pledge Drive," in which Elaine's boss unwrapped a Snickers Bar. He placed the candy bar on a plate and ate it using a knife and fork during an office business meeting. So, yeah. In the Seinfeld show, the knife and fork incident sparked a social awareness on Manhattan Island in which "the smart people" began to use various cutlery to eat candy in order not to touch the candy with their fingers (such as eating M&Ms with a tablespoon).

Perhaps human trends begin with the peculiar habit of an individual. Web search, "Ten innovations that built ancient Rome." You may be surprised by some of the underpinnings of Rome, a world-class empire that rose and lasted more than one thousand years. I was surprised to see

> She had a peanut butter cup too. With the spoon, she scooped peanut butter out of the cup, enough to cover the first quarter of the tip of the spoon on the concave side.

the welfare system listed, and that some attribute it to hastening Rome's eventual downfall. In the United States, we have a welfare system today that is expanding beyond both government control and the capability of the workforce to sustain it.

Cultural assimilation did not make the top ten list. Beginning with the province of Greece, the Romans took the time to assimilate Greek practices that they believed to work well, and to attempt to revise those that did not work well. Then, they invited the Greeks to participate in the newly remodeled culture. This

worked, and the practice continued every time the Romans acquired a new province (kingdoms that either capitulated or were defeated in combat). This system of government was complex, but it did expand and the Roman civilization endured well beyond any previous civilization. Graft, greed, decreasing confidence in government, and a failing moral compass among the Roman citizens contributed heavily to the empire breaking, and the return of the broken pieces to their tribal origins.

So, what was the missing detail about the young lady who ate her banana with a spoon? She had a peanut butter cup too. With the spoon, she scooped peanut butter out of the cup, enough to cover the first quarter of the tip of the spoon on the concave side. Then, she used the remaining space of the concave side of the spoon to carve out a piece of the banana. So, she actually ate banana and peanut butter in a single bite, with style and grace, avoiding getting food on her hands. Genius. So far, I have detected no popular trend to do what she did.

Find Tony's published novels online at https://wp.me/P9ep8b-1D

See and comment on a novel being written with blog posts at Tony's Website and Blog: https://writeathriller.wordpress.com/

Participate in the writing of Tony's 5th novel as a series of blog posts at the website. Readers and writers are invited to comment anonymously on each blog post. Experience the great game of crafting a novel today. #TAG1writer

Source: EzineArticles

Sherbet is a drink which was very popular in Ottoman, South Asia, Caucasus and the Balkans yet it remains as popular today as it was 300 years ago in Turkey, Central Asia, Balkans and some parts of Middle East.

Taste joy after every sip

Could sherbet be the new drink of the UK?
Makam looks partners to join the UK market
with its Ottoman drink, Sherbet

By DAN PETERS
July 8, 2022
London

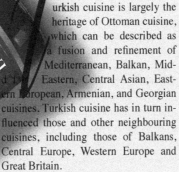

Turkish cuisine is largely the heritage of Ottoman cuisine, which can be described as a fusion and refinement of Mediterranean, Balkan, Middle Eastern, Central Asian, Eastern European, Armenian, and Georgian cuisines. Turkish cuisine has in turn influenced those and other neighbouring cuisines, including those of Balkans, Central Europe, Western Europe and Great Britain.

The Ottomans fused various culinary traditions of their realm with influences from Mesopotamian cuisine, Greek cuisine, Levantine cuisine, Egyptian cuisine, Balkan cuisine, along with traditional Turkic elements from Central Asia such as ayran and kaymak, creating a vast array of specialities. Sherbet is one of them. Turkish cuisine, which dominates the British market, is unthinkable without an Ottoman shebet, in which this situation appears as a shortcoming situation. Sherbet is a drink which was very popular in Ottoman, South Asia, Caucasus and the Balkans yet it remains as popular today as it was 300 years ago in Turkey, Central Asia, Balkans and some parts of Middle East.

Sherbet has been reserved for special occasions, and has been popular during the month of Ramadan and it is served in large crystal bowls and is enjoyed after sunset to break the day's fast. In rural areas of both western and eastern Turkey, Sherbet is still a popular drink yet it is mostly home made and should drink it in a day, doesn't last months even weeks and not good for trade. Yet, an enterprise in Bursa, where is a city of North Western in Turkey produces sherbets for trade.

Along with its refreshing taste, Ottoman sherbet health benefits are a lot, which includles helping to lower cholesterol, weight management and regulating blood pressure. It makes skin smoother and is very effective in removing radiation from the body. Sherbet is a blend of many fruits and spices, which makes it a remarkable antioxidant, as well.

The company Makam, located in Bursa, the city in the North Easter of Turkiye, produces types of possible sherbet flavors, some of the most popular include date basil, date rose, tamarind (demirhindi), mandarin and pomegranate, planning to produce sherbet in the UK market and look for franchises. "The market is stable and strong in the UK. Turkish, Balkans and Middle East restaurants itself a huge market for the Sherber." Mr. Ayhan Yasan, CEO of ExpoTurk Group Companies said in a statement last week, and he underlined that we've been looking for partners to distribute our variety of sherbets and other drinks.

Desire meets taste.

Along with its refreshing taste, Ottoman sherbet health benefits are a lot, which includles helping to lower cholesterol, weight management and regulating blood pressure. It makes skin smoother and is very effective in removing radiation from the body.

makamicecekleri
makamsarayicecekleri
makamicecek.com.tr /makamicecek

MEDIA AND RESTAURANT BUSINESS

By F. ONCU
7 July 2022
London

LONDON - I involved either partly or directly many interviews with very successful Entrepreneurs. All these figures are the masters in their fields. I figure out something common in them; strong relations with the media. Ms. Emma, Heathcote-James, Founder/CEO Little Soap Company, Winner of Queen's Enterprise Award 2022, was one of them. I asked Emma what is the secret of her success comes? Her answer was remarkable; "I say Yes to Press! It doesn't matter what you are talking about – people will just remember you and the product. I would always say yes to news items."

Last month, when we decided to release a magazine, covers food and restaurant business, I decided to visit some restaurants in Royal Leamington Spa on a Tuesday evening, not a good day for most of the restaurants because it is either Monday or Tuesday. Yes, I was not wrong, almost all of them were no customers but one, Giggling Squid, a Thai Restaurant in Royal Priors Shopping Center on Recent Street. When I first see it from outside I thought there is something going on.

As I was walking towards the restaurant door with excited eyes, a waiter scratched me at the door. Please wait, she replied as soon as I said that I'm a journalist and would like to see the manager. Seconds later, he showed up outside of the restaurant and asked me how he can help me. As soon as I asked him what is going on here, and why the restaurant is full this evening, he replied; "We're like this almost every day. Of course, our course makes the difference yet the point is how we tell the people living in Leamington Spa and neighboring towns. Media is the solution. I do have all the contacts of media outlets in the town and around. We stay in touch with them and see them here most of the year. Sometime we get reviews and shares on social media. Publicity helps us to reach people here and around."

Media has been a powerful tool to influence people positively and negatively. Today, we live under the power of media as a source of information, communication and entertainment that enhance the knowledge of us through the different types of news or events in our daily lives.

It is a commination theory that "if you watch television more than two hours a day, your mentality would be televised mentality. You act and behave as you get form the television." This theory is told back to 50s. Today our mind is shaped by the tools of mass communication consist of television, radio, newspapers, magazines and internet such as : Facebook, Twitter, YouTube, Instagram, Google and other social networking channels. It simply means that media has the power to give information and provide an easy means of communication among people.

Media is a powerful and trusted tool among people living developed countries like the UK, US and EU. Here are some facts;

FACTS ABOUT MEDIA

· 81% of consumers' purchasing decisions are influenced by their friends' social media posts. (Forbes)

· 66% of consumers have been inspired to purchase from a new brand after seeing media images from other consumers (Stackla)

· Consumers are 71% more likely to

You and/or your business have been a sourse of news, reviews and photos for media .

❝ Conversions increase 133% when mobile shoppers see positive reviews before buying. (Bazaarvoice)

make a purchase based on media referrals. (Hubspot)

Conversions increase 133% when mobile shoppers see positive reviews before buying. (Bazaarvoice)

78% of consumers say companies' media posts impact their purchases. (Forbes)

56% of consumers say they're more influenced by media images and videos when online shopping now than they were before the pandemic (Stackla)

WHAT TO DO?

Depending on your business, lets say restaurant, there are many ways to make your food or items a news. You have a fancy restaurant, you're the only restaurant cooks and serves the steak, pizza and desserts. Yet many are not aware of it. Like many other businesses, restaurant business has parts. Media relation is one of them. Here are some of the things you should do;

Web page. Having an attractive, professional website is the best way to stand out from the competition. A good effective website helps build a strong online presence and helps communicate quality information to not just your consumers but media.

Make your webpage media friendly. Your webpage should have a "Press Room" page which should covers press releases, high quality images and recipes of some dishes you serve. Historical information about some of the dishes you have and news about people like political figures, artists, teams visited your restaurant. Reviews from customers and media should be in press room page as well.

Press release. Write a press release whenever find a reason like grand opening, seasonal opening, special dishes for special days like Christmas, Father's Day, Mothers Days, Valentina's Day or any new dishes you just started serving. The press release should include the atmosphere of your restaurant, lighting, location, ambiance and some of the reviews from costumers.

Local Media. Search and collect the list of any local media and contact the editors. Invite them to your restaurant for some reasons like press conference, introducing your new dish, or something about your restaurant contributes such as event, party or something like that.

National Media. Search and collect the list of national media, reviews restaurants and specializes in restaurant, food business. Contact The New York Times Restaurant Review editor if you are assertive about your cuisine, your services and the ambiance of your restaurant.

Stay with both local and national media editors in touch and send them press releases occasionally. They will eventually write a review or talk about your restaurant either on their media or social media.

Reviews. Be active on review sites, magazines and newspapers. As Bazaar Voice stated that conversions increase 133% when mobile shoppers see positive reviews before buying. Media reviews are most affective tools to bring costumers to your restaurant. Most customers read reviews before dining at the restaurant. So, reviews must be answered and managed. They can make or break your brand. Being proactive on reviews, both good and negative, is an excellent way to promote your restaurant.

Grand opening. Organize a grand opening all the time. If you open a new restaurant or branch that is a good opportunity to invite media, local political figures, artists and some of your loyal customers. If not a new restaurant or branch, do a season's opening, celebration or find a reason to invite these figures.

Celebrate. Celebrate your contacts birthday, holiday seasons, anniversaries etc. Send them a card or message. Invite them for a coffe or dessert.

Get Awards. Be an award-winning even be multi award-winning entrepreneur or company. There are many organizations willing to give awards. Register and be a member. There are also many events going on, join and get your awards. Than use these awards as a slogan when market your business; "Multi Award-Winning……"

Social Media. Social media is a part of mass media. Use and update them effectively. Social media has become the most influential and important virtual space where the platform is not only used for social networking but is also a great way of digitally advertising your brand and your products.

Loyal Customers. Don't neglect your loyal customers. Offer them something for free which could be tea, coffee, dessert and so on. They are ambassadors of your restaurant. Some of them may have contacts in media and some other channels.

Build Your Media. It's not just social media, it's a new media as well. Treath them you're the media patron and those are your media channels. Brotcast live events, news, conduct interviews through YouTube, Instagram and other channels. Build your own magazine. Newyox's state-of-art service enables people to get their own magazines with an affordable prices. The cost is low yet the effect is high. The magazines, Newyox creates, are available both print and electronic all over the globe in 190 countries and over 40.000 networks, platform, retailers and libries including Amazon, Barnes&Noble, Chapters&Indigo, Rakuten, Blackwell's, and Waterstones.

As a result, keep in touch with media is an essential part of your success not just in restaurant business but many other businesses. Whenever a new movie or a book released, they highlight what the media said. Whenever a new show starts, they highlight what media said. So, it's extremely important what media says about your restaurant, cuisine, desserts and ambiance.

ABOUT THE AUTHOR

Fatih Oncu is Founder and Director of Newyox, a London-based multi-sided media platform creates opportunities for publishers. He is also a publisher of a few magazines including The Reader's House, Entrepreneur Prime and London Taste.

He has over 20 years of experience in media, plus 10 years of education in Journalism at the College of Saint Rose (BA), Publishing at NYU (MS) and Digital Transformation at MIT (EP)

Buffet

The pricing of the buffet menu in the Best Buffet Restaurants is tailored to provide opportunities to customers for enjoying diverse cuisines and delicacies without making a dent in their budgets.

BY SHAHI MASALA

The Best Buffet RESTAURANTS

Buffet dining emerged in the 16th century in France and has continued to develop into the favorite alternative for a large base of restaurant customers. The Best Buffet Restaurants that have emerged over the course of time have not only reformed the conventional benchmarks of restaurant dining but have also provided the opportunity for flexible modification of the operations of a restaurant.

For example, restaurants which have higher customer visits or those which provide catering services can utilize buffet as a promising means for feeding the large base of visiting guests. Furthermore, buffets have been utilized as promising approaches for the promotion of restaurants or celebrating special occasions.

Types of buffets

The following types of buffets are generally found in some of the Best Buffet Restaurants and could be selected according to the requirements of the customer.

Cafeteria style:

In this type of buffet, customers are required to select plates of food according to their choice while waiting in a queue. The cafeteria-style buffet is less frequently practised in restaurants.

All You Can Eat:

The name says it all! These buffet styles are considered as the most beneficial investments on behalf of the cus-tomers as they would have to pay a single price for serving themselves with a wide assortment of delicacies. However, it is interesting to note that the popularity of All You Can Eat buffets is waning due to the increasing threats of obesity.

Healthy Buffets:

These concepts are followed by restaurants that provide soups, fresh produce and salad bars in their menus and promote healthy eating habits. However, these could not be considered as one of the Best Buffet Restaurants owing to the criticisms on the basis of the higher calorie content of specific menu items.

Catered buffets:

The catered buffets approach is followed by restaurants which specialize in business meetings, special occasions, and weddings as well as holiday parties and also involve facilities of off-site catered buffets in certain cases.

Pros and Cons of restaurant buffets

While it is explicitly observed that the Best Buffet Restaurants have changed the way people looked at dining alongside reforming the traditional approaches followed in the restaurant business, it is also important to focus on the positive as well as negative sides to buffet restaurants.

·Restaurants could leverage the benefit of minimal workforce required for conducting buffets. Furthermore, a lot of customers could be served at once thereby implying the promising opportunities for higher income.

·Buffets serve as promotional tactics and can be used to lure in customers who would not have dined at a restaurant otherwise due to budget concerns.

·The pricing of the buffet menu in the Best Buffet Restaurants is tailored to provide opportunities to customers for enjoying diverse cuisines and delicacies without making a dent in their budgets.

·On the contrary, restaurants also face limitations especially in terms of profit margins as buffets generally cost less than the conventional sit-down dinner.

·Buffets are also associated with the concerns of maintaining food safety, aesthetic appeal and overall maintenance.

Despite the trivial setbacks, buffet restaurants continue to explore new opportunities in the restaurant market with more and more restaurant owners implementing innovation in their buffet offerings through the pairing of food and drinks along with distinct presentations. (EzineArticles)

Do These 5 Important Steps Before You Start
GRILLING

Once you start grilling, you would want to focus on cooking

Grill in an open area of your yard, away from any flammable objects like walls or trees. Always check your grease tray and empty it out to prevent a grease fire. Wear gloves, use long handled tongs and keep a fire extinguisher nearby.

BY
ADRIAN T.
CHENG

As with traditional cooking, preparation is paramount when you're about to cook your food on the grill. Getting everything ready and checking your gear will save you a lot of time and energy once you start your fire. Once you start grilling, you would want to focus on cooking your food perfectly and not be distracted by other things.

Here are 5 important steps to take before you start grilling:

Prepare your grates

It's important to prep your grates before putting any food on them. This will prolong the life

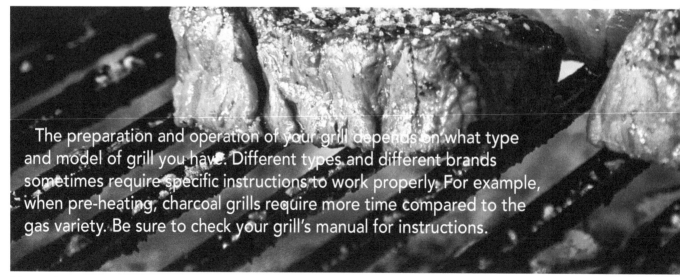

The preparation and operation of your grill depends on what type and model of grill you have. Different types and different brands sometimes require specific instructions to work properly. For example, when pre-heating, charcoal grills require more time compared to the gas variety. Be sure to check your grill's manual for instructions.

It's important to prep your grates before putting any food on them. This will prolong the life of your grates by keeping rust off. Do this every time before using your grill.

of your grates by keeping rust off. Do this every time before using your grill.

If your grill is brand new, spray the grates with high heat cooking spray evenly before turning on the grill. Turn on the grill to medium heat until the oil starts to smoke and burns off. If you're using old grates, pre-heat your grill then brush off any debris.

Prioritize safety

Anything that has to do with fire and high temperatures should be done with caution, and grilling is no exception. To avoid accidents, you should prioritize safety by practicing caution every time you grill at home.

Grill in an open area of your yard, away from any flammable objects like walls or trees. Always check your grease tray and empty it out to prevent a grease fire. Wear gloves, use long handled tongs and keep a fire extinguisher nearby.

Prepare the food beforehand

Once you turn on your grill to pre-heat it, your food should be ready to go. You won't want to be going back and forth from your kitchen to your grill while cooking. To save time and energy, prepare your food beforehand - slice and cut up your meats and veggies and make the sauces.

Don't forget to bring out clean plates, grilling accessories, a food thermometer, paper towels and trash bags along with your food.

Pay attention to your grill

The preparation and operation of your grill depends on what type and model of grill you have. Different types and different brands sometimes require specific instructions to work properly. For example, when pre-heating, charcoal grills require more time compared to the gas variety. Be sure to check your grill's manual

for instructions.

Check and maintain your grill

For successful barbecues, you should make it a habit to always check your grill. Maintenance is also a must. Brush your grates, check your grease trap often, check your propane tank, and keep your grill in a covered area for storage, preferably with a cover.

Do these 5 important steps before grilling for a successful cookout!

Adrian T. Cheng is a food blogger and a BBQ expert. Through years of barbecue experience, reviewing various grilling accessories and trying delicious and unique recipes, he is sharing his knowledge with everyone through his blog. For more grilling secrets, tips, recipes and more, head over to Adrian's website where he has other interesting grill-related products and posts. (EzineArticles)

Photo by Gonzalo Guzman

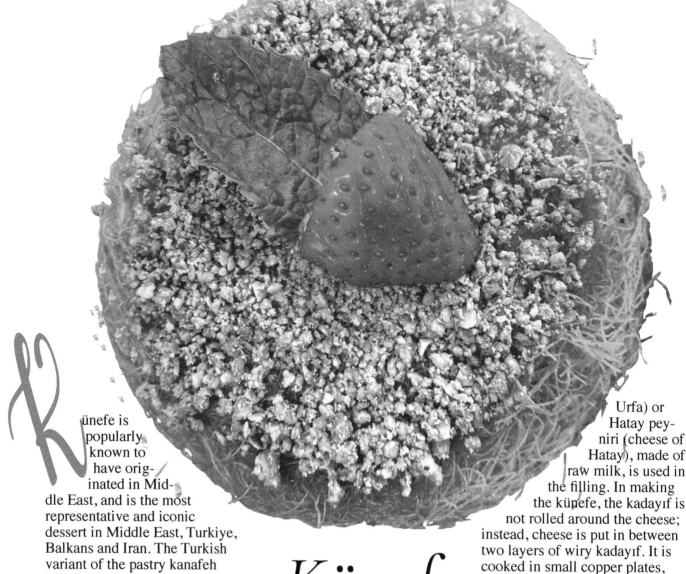

Künefe is popularly known to have originated in Middle East, and is the most representative and iconic dessert in Middle East, Turkiye, Balkans and Iran. The Turkish variant of the pastry kanafeh is called kunefe and 'Turkish Künefe is a crispy, cheese-filled dessert made with 'kadayıf'.(half baked string- shaped dough)

Kunefe is a popular and traditional Turkish dessert made with spun pastry called kataifi, soaked in a sweet, sugar-based syrup called attar, and typically layered with cheese, or with other ingredients such as clotted cream, pistachio or nuts, depending on your choice. It is popular in the Turkiye, Persuan and Arab world, particularly Egypt and the Levant. Variants are also found in Greece, and the Balkans.

In the Hatay region of Turkey, which is a neighbour city of Syrian border and has a large Arab population, the pastry is called künefe and the wiry shreds are called tel kadayıf. A semi-soft cheese such as Urfa peyniri (cheese of

Künefe POWER

Sofra, an authentic Turkish restaurant serves Kunefe, in Mayfair at the heart of city. Its sweet comes seperatly that makes the Kunefe light or heavy. It is good for those who love dessert but should stay away...

Urfa) or Hatay peyniri (cheese of Hatay), made of raw milk, is used in the filling. In making the künefe, the kadayıf is not rolled around the cheese; instead, cheese is put in between two layers of wiry kadayıf. It is cooked in small copper plates, and then served very hot in syrup with clotted cream (kaymak) and topped with pistachios or walnuts. In the Turkish cuisine, there is also yassı kadayıf and ekmek kadayıfı, none of which is made of wiry shreds.

it is rare to find a restaurant in the Uk even in the Europe, that specializes making a kadayif. But you're lucy if you live in or visiting London, because there are some restaurants serve Künefe. Sofra, located in Mayfair, is one of them.

Künefe is hard to prepare, so it's almost never made at home. Most people wait until they eat at a kebab house to enjoy the authentic dessert, yet as I said, it is almost impossible to find and eat if you live outside of London or Europe, I could say even in Newyork, as being a New Yorker for 10 years.

GREAT FOOD FAST
by Martha Stewart Living Magazine

ABOUT MARTHA STEWART LIVING MAGAZINE

Martha Stewart Living was first published in 1990. Since then, more than two dozen books have been published by the magazine's editors. Martha Stewart is the author of dozens of best-selling books on cooking, entertaining, gardening, weddings, and decorating. She…More about Martha Stewart Living Magazine

Designed in a contemporary and easy-to-read format, Everyday Food boasts lush, full-color photography and plenty of suggestions for substitutions and variations.

No matter how busy you are, at the end of the day you want fresh, flavorful meals that are easy to prepare. And you want lots of choices and variations—recipes that call for your favorite foods and take advantage of excellent (and readily available) ingredients. In the first book from the award-winning magazine Everyday Food, you'll find all of that: 250 simple recipes for delicious meals that are quick enough to make any day of the week.

Because a change in weather affects how we cook as much as what we cook, the recipes in Everyday Food are arranged by season. For spring, you'll find speedy preparations for main-course salads, chicken, and poached salmon that minimize time spent at the stove; summer features quick techniques for grilling the very best burgers and kabobs as well as no-cook pasta sauces; for fall, there are braised meats and hearty main-course soups; and winter provides new takes on rich one-dish meals, roasts and stews, and hearty baked pastas. Finally, a chapter on basics explains how to make year-round staples such as foolproof roast chicken, risotto, couscous, and chocolate sauce.

Designed in a contemporary and easy-to-read format, Everyday Food boasts lush, full-color photography and plenty of suggestions for substitutions and variations. With Everyday Food, even the busiest on-the-go cook can look forward to meals that bring freshness, nutrition, and a range of flavors to dinner all week long.

Paperback
$24.99
Mar 13, 2007
ISBN
9780307354167

FAST FOOD AND
CALORIES

BY
KAREN
SESSIONS

Isn't it oddly shocking that America is so well-advanced in everything, except health and fitness? While the fitness industry tells us to count calories and exercise for fat loss, we grow fatter and fatter as a nation.

Here in the technology and information age,Guest Posting we have more knowledge and advancements than ever before in history. Sixty years ago, who would have ever thought that you could send an instant message over a phone, let alone take a picture with it? Sixty years ago, who would have thought we would be capable of sending a man to the moon, but fail the war on obesity and cancer?

Isn't it oddly shocking that America is so well-advanced in everything except health and fitness? While the fitness industry tells us to count calories and exercise for fat loss, we grow fatter and fatter as a nation.

Running parallel to the fitness industry is the fast food chains, doing their best to keep on the top of "healthy eating" trend. It seems the fast-food industry can tailor to anyone's dieting needs with "fat-free," "low-calorie," and "low-carb" menu items.

Today, fast food is considered a normal eating venture among the average person. People aren't just eating out on special occasions or weekends anymore; they are eating out all the time. But is it the calories in fast food that's so destructive to the body and waistline or does the problem lie deeper?

Fast Food and Obesity

Fast food is simply tasty, ready-cooked meals packed to go. Fast food has been around since the early 1900's, but its popularity sparked and grew in the 1940's with the birth of good ole' Mickey D's; quick food priced cheaply. Within a few years similar fast-food operations popped up everywhere in the blink of an eye.

With the compelling rise in fast-food restaurants since the 1940's, oddly, too, started the rise in obesity and cancer during that same time period. It doesn't take a rocket scientist to do the math and link fast food to the obesity and cancer crisis.

Fast Food and its Nutritional Value

To say fast food has a "nutritional value" is an oxymoron. There is absolutely nothing nutritional about fast food. Fast food simply feeds hunger and/or your immediate craving. Fast food does not feed your body in the form of usable lasting energy or building materials, the essence your body thrives on for life itself.

Fast food is highly processed with a wide array of additives. The concept of fast food is obviously, food ready-to-eat and served quickly. To ensure fast food's low cost to the consumer, the fast food products are made with highly-processed ingredients to give it shelf-life, to hold consistency, and to enhance flavor. Fast food is altered from its original healthy form it was meant to nourish the body with, to a denatured form that lacks any nutritional value whatsoever.

According to Diana Schwarzbein, M.D., "The FDA Total Diet Study found that fast-food hamburgers, across the board, contained 113 different pesticide residues." So my question is why does the FDA want to regulate the sale of vitamins, minerals, and herbs that are actually beneficial for the body when there's a linking fast-food / cancer / obesity crisis on our hands?

Why Fast Food is Fattening and Dangerous

Wake up people. It's not the calories in fast food that's damaging to your health and waistline, it's the chemical additives such as aspartame and MSG (monosodium glutamate). These chemical additives are approved by the FDA and studies show that they lead to weight and disease issues.

Synthetic chemicals added to processed food, including fast food, damage your body's cells. Your body is made up of nutrients found in plants and animals you eat. Man-made food items loaded with pesticides, as well as aspartame, margarine, and other man-made chemicals do not nourish your body. If your body can't use what you put into it you will gain fat and decrease health.

Since we can't visually see what actually happens at the molecular level when we eat processed food, we discount it and rely on the FDA to do our thinking for us. After all, if its FDA approved, it MUST be okay to eat, right? Not at all.

Nutrients from the food we eat allow us to burn fat and be healthy. Your body cannot process synthetic chemicals. If a food item can't be processed, it will end up lodged in areas of your body, primarily fatty areas and tissues, creating an acidic pH.

A simple fast-food chicken breast can contain everything from modified corn starch to hydrolyzed corn gluten. Hello? Chicken comprised of corn? A fast-food chicken nugget is nearly 60% corn, and corn is what farmers use to fatten up cattle.

Michael Pollan, author of, The Omnivore's Dilemma says it perfectly – "How did we ever get to a point where we need investigative journalist to tell us where our food comes from?"

A good visual that Dr. Mark A. Gustafson found is that it takes fifty-one days to digest fast food chicken nuggets or French fries. FIFTY-ONE DAYS! Does that sound healthy? I could care less about the caloric, fat, or carbohydrate content. That's not the problem, people. The problem with fast food is that it's void of nutrients and loaded with chemicals not recognized by the body.

What's even more devastating is the book The Fast Food Diet written by Stephan Sinatra, M.D. This is a sad state when a doctor promotes eating chemically-altered food with addictive chemicals and damaged fats that scars the artery walls and contribute to total metabolic damage.

Eating Good and Avoiding the Hidden Dangers

Granted, calories do count to an extent, but what counts more is the quality of the calorie. If you want to lose fat then you have to change your eating habits. This doesn't mean opt for Healthy Choice® and Smart One's® frozen meals because they appear to be healthy. Food manufacturers use deceptive marking tactics to create an illusion to make people buy their product.

To lose fat and keep it off you should choose foods in their natural state, such as fresh organic cuts of meat, fresh organic fruits and vegetables, essential fats, and plenty of filtered water. It's vital that you go back to the basics.

Make eating fresh and organic food choices the bulk of your diet. If you do that, you will never have to count calories again. The quality of food outweighs the quantity every time.

References: Schwarbein, Diana M.D. The Schwarzbein Principle. 1999. 287 Pollan, Michael. The Omnivore's Dilemma. 2006. 1 (ArticlesFactory)

MI COCINA
RECIPES AND RAPTURE FROM MY KITCHEN IN MEXICO: A COOKBOOK
By Rick Martínez

NEW YORK TIMES BESTSELLER • A highly personal love letter to the beauty and bounty of México in more than 100 transportive recipes, from the beloved food writer and host of the Babish Culinary Universe show Pruébalo on YouTube and Food52's Sweet Heat

"This intimate look at a country's cuisine has as much spice as it does soul." — Publishers Weekly (starred review)

ONE OF THE MOST ANTICIPATED COOKBOOKS OF 2022 — Time, Food52

Hardcover
$35.00
May 03, 2022
ISBN
9780593138700

Join Rick Martínez on a once-in-a-lifetime culinary journey throughout México that begins in Mexico City and continues through 32 states, in 156 cities, and across 20,000 incredibly delicious miles. In Mi Cocina, Rick shares deeply personal recipes as he re-creates the dishes and specialties he tasted throughout his journey. Inspired by his travels, the recipes are based on his taste memories and experiences. True to his spirit and reflective of his deep connections with people and places, these dishes will revitalize your pantry and transform your cooking repertoire.

Highlighting the diversity, richness, and complexity of Mexican cuisine, he includes recipes like herb and cheese meatballs bathed in a smoky, spicy chipotle sauce from Oaxaca called Albóndigas en Chipotle; northern México's grilled Carne Asada that he stuffs into a grilled quesadilla for full-on cheesy-meaty food euphoria; and tender sweet corn tamales packed with succulent shrimp, chiles, and roasted tomatoes from Sinaloa on the west coast. Rick's poignant essays throughout lend context — both personal and cultural — to quilt together a story that is rich and beautiful, touching and insightful.

ABOUT THE AUTHOR

Rick Martínez is the host of the companion video series Mi Cocina and Sweet Heat, both on the Food52 YouTube channel and Pruébalo on the Babish Culinary Universe channel. He cohosts the Borderline Salty podcast with Carla Lalli Music, is a regular contributor The New York Times, and teaches live, weekly cooking classes for the Food Network Kitchen. He currently resides in Mazatlán with his dog, Choco, where he cooks, eats, and enjoys the Mexican Pacific coast.

AFFILIATE MARKETING SECRETS

WHAT I WISH I KNEW BEFORE!

BY
TIM
HALLORAN

There's high ticket products which have a much larger value. A high ticket product sale can earn you the same as by selling hundreds of the lower value item.

The affiliate marketing secrets I'm sharing here aren't really "secrets" to some affiliates. But for me, when I started affiliate marketing back in the early 2000's, they would have been useful to know about. It would have saved me several years of hard work if I would have known about these factors in an affiliate business.

I spent a huge amount of time trying out bad strategies and promoting low paying products. It was immensely frustrating not only to struggle getting results as an affiliate, but when they did eventually come to see such tiny little commissions that it was hardly worth all that struggle!

The fist insight I'm going to share is to get an email autoresponder. An auto-responder is a software which allows affiliates to collect emails from a website and automate the delivery of email messages to your list.

For a long time I didn't have an auto-responder. I simply tried to get people to my websites and sell affiliate products directly from there. But there's a problem in that customers will often need several contact points before they purchase something. So a single landing on a website will seldom generate a sale. On a website, a visitor only has a small window of opportunity to make a buying decision. But once you get your visitors email information, you can extend this time period by months, years and even decades!

You can give them many more "touch points" with which to showcase your offerings, give value and help your subscribers with whatever issue they are facing.

The next issue I faced was choosing the affiliate products which I would sell. The products I chose as an affiliate were those which I would have bought myself. This is a good policy because you can more easily create content around something you're interested in. But I choose low value products and used affiliate programs which paid the least! I didn't know this was an issue till much later when I discovered subscription affiliate programs which paid ongoing commissions for each sale.

With a low value product from eBay or Amazon, for example, you only get tiny amounts - usually less than 10% commission. Digital products pay more like 30%-50% commission. Then there's high ticket products which have a much larger value. A high ticket product sale can earn you the same as by selling hundreds of the lower value item.

With a product range you can benefit from subscription products, one off commissions and high ticket sales. In addition to this you can also benefit from a built in sales team, who close sales on your behalf. With most affiliate products, you refer a sale and only get paid once. So you need to continue selling more and more products. With subscription and high ticket, you can continue earning from your referrals, potentially for years. So the same work is rewarded much more with such a strategy.

Another huge benefit of using such a product range is that paid marketing strategies are much more within reach. I struggled with free marketing tactics, making sporadic sales which amounted to very little income. With a high ticket product range, it's much easier to make a profit while running paid marketing.

Plus, once you're profitable, and are running paid advertising campaigns, you can scale up quickly. Simply increase marketing budget! With organic and cheaper marketing strategies, this is much more difficult. I was struggling for years because I was selling low value products and using free marketing strategies which couldn't be scaled up!

Another affiliate marketing secret which I didn't discover until a few years of struggle is to get help. Back in the early 2000's it was far more difficult to build an online business from scratch. You needed more technical know-how. You needed to be able to build websites yourself. Today software takes much of the technical wizardry out of building online business. You can press a couple of buttons and have a ready made website up and running in minutes. You can also join a group of other affiliates which can help enormously with your mindset and personal growth.

Going it alone as an affiliate is tough, especially when well meaning family members and friends are trying to talk you out of it, and telling you that it's a scam! Once in a community of online entrepreneurs, my confidence grew. I was able to ask questions and get things done more easily. Other people had similar questions to me, and joining groups where coaches and mentors were on hand shortened the learning curve.

Most of all joining a community of online business owners helped me believe that I could build an income from affiliate marketing. Before this I struggled with mindset issues and lack of confidence. If you doubt you're going in the right direction, it's much easier to quit, or dawdle. It's easier to procrastinate and lose your direction.

To sum up, these are my affiliate marketing secrets:

1. Get an autoresponder - an email marketing service made a huge difference to my affiliate business

2. Use subscription products, high ticket products and a product range, rather than low value products which only offer single commissions

3. Get help - join an online community where you can build trust with a coach, find accountability partners and get questions answered.

Affiliate marketing is a tough business to crack and the drop out rate is around 95%. Remember the reason you're doing it and find a good program and stick to it.

Tim Halloran is a stuntman and online entrepreneur. He has created an online resource to help new and struggling affiliates: http://affiliatemarketingmentorsonline.com

SOURCE: AFFILIATE MARKETING MENTORS ONLINE

BUSINESS BOOK

ELITE MINDS
by Stan Beecham

Whether you're a self starter, team player, or corporate leader, you can apply these proven mind techniques to any field or endeavor— quickly, easily, and effectively.

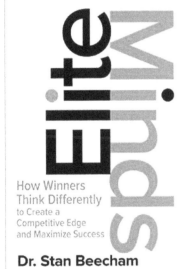

How Winners Think Differently to Create a Competitive Edge and Maximize Success

Dr. Stan Beecham

ELITE MINDS THINK ALIKE. Discover the winning secrets of the world's most successful people.

Discover the winning secrets of the world's most successful people.

As a top-level sport psychologist and performance consultant, Dr. Stan Beeham knows what it takes to succeed—on the playing field, in the board room, and in all aspects of life. This award-winning book takes you inside the minds of major-league athletes, Olympic medal winners, and world-class business leaders to reveal the key motivators and mental processes that drive people to victory. Learn how to:

RETRAIN YOUR BRAIN to think like a winner.

CONQUER YOUR FEARS and go after your goals.

ACHIEVE PEAK PERFOR-MANCE and reach your full potential.

BECOME WHO YOU WANT TO BE mentally, physically, personally and professionally.

Whether you're a self starter, team player, or corporate leader, you can apply these proven mind techniques to any field or endeavor—quickly, easily, and effectively. Filled with power-boosting mental exercises, positive attitude adjusters, and inspiring true stories of individual success, the book provides all the tools you need to set your goals, sharpen your focus, and achieve your personal best. It's like having your own private coach cheering you on every step of the way. If you can think it, you can do it—with the game-changing power of Elite Minds.

Winner of the Benjamin Franklin Award—Updated and Expanded Edition

ABOUT THE AUTHOR

Dr. Stan Beecham is a Sport Psychologist and Leadership Consultant based in Roswell, Georgia. Legendary Coach Vince Dooley gave Beecham his start as an undergraduate student at UGA allowing him to work with Kevin Butler, the great college and professional kicker for the Chicago Bears.

Dooley later hired Dr. Beecham to start the Sport Psychology Program for the Athletic Department. He was instrumental in helping UGA win numerous individual and team championships during his tenure.

Today his work with collegiate, Olympic and Professional athletes from many sports has afforded him an insight into the minds of great competitors that only few have had the good fortune to gain.

Dr. Beecham has taken his wisdom into the business world as he develops and creates leadership development programs for corporate clientsA world-class speaker and presenter, Dr. Beecham shares his vast knowledge and experience in this incredible work

Explore the Flavors and Health Benefits of Indian Cuisine at Home

Creating delicious Indian foods at home is now possible for anyone, regardless of their culinary skills. With the right shortcuts, you can prepare nutritious meals in less time.

In the last few years, more Americans have gotten hooked on the rich, mouth-watering flavors and bold spices of South Asian cuisine. In fact, research has shown an increase in searches for Indian cuisine, making it the second most searched for cuisine on Instagram.

Creating delicious Indian foods at home is now possible for anyone, regardless of their culinary skills. With the right shortcuts, you can prepare nutritious meals in less time. Ready to get started? Here are three reasons why you should add Indian cuisine to your lunch and dinner rotations:

1. It's better for you: Indian cuisine features a number of ingredients that support a healthy lifestyle. For example, lentils are an excellent source of protein and gut-friendly fiber, leaving you feeling fuller for longer. Commonly used spices, such as cumin and ginger, aid in digestion and provide anti-inflammatory benefits.

Research has shown an increase in searches for Indian cuisine, making it the second most searched for cuisine on Instagram.

And if you stick to vegetarian and vegan dishes, you'll be taking it a step further. Plant-based diets not only taste great, but have been linked to weight loss, better blood sugar control and a decreased risk of heart disease, among other health benefits.

2. It's better for the planet: Eating a plant-based diet is one of the simplest ways to protect the planet. With its wide variety of protein-rich dishes and flavorful ingredients, Indian cuisine is a go-to choice for anyone looking to cut back on meat. Studies show that if you eat one plant-based meal a day for a year, you'll save almost 200,000 gallons of water – that's equivalent to 11,400 showers.

3. Time-saving meal kits can make it convenient: For people who are not sure how to get started, a meal kit subscription is the perfect way to gain fluency in Indian flavors and makes the experience of putting authentic dishes on the table easy.

In particular, The Cumin Club, available nationwide, offers more than 30 authentic Indian dishes starting at $4.99 each. All you need is hot water and about five minutes to make a satisfying meal. This better-for-you option uses all-natural ingredients you can feel good about, including spices sourced from different regions of India. From classic street food to comforting bowls of paneer butter masala, the brand's ever-expanding menu is vegetarian-and vegan-friendly, represents various cuisines of India, and is an excellent choice for busy, health-conscious foodies on a budget. To learn more, visit thecuminclub.com and receive 20% off your first order by using the code: EAT20.

Making authentic Indian food a part of your weekly rotation is an easy way to add healthier options with a ton of flavor. Thanks to new shortcuts, preparing it at home is easier than ever.

(StatePoint)

Tips To Buying Best Juicers

BY
CUMBA
GOWRI

There is a way to get more juice out of greens even with a centrifugal appliance. Tightly wrap the leaves in a cylindrical roll, either around a piece of carrot or ginger, or on its own and feed it through the feed tube.

Some facts about juicing machines -

Heating and oxidation are the twin culprits which cause the destruction of nutrients in juice. The juice extracted by using a slow machine is more nutritious and contains vitamins, enzymes and minerals which otherwise lost to heating effects and agitation effects in a centrifugal juicing machine.

Due to the slow speed, nutrition is not lost and also ensures the longer shelf life of juice along with retaining original flavors of the extracted liquids.

The AMZchef masticating machine has a very modern design which helps it to fit in with any decor or design of a modern kitchen. With its standout color it adds a touch of glamor to the kitchen.

Due to sturdy material used in construction of the machine it can resist corrosion and any warp due to heating. It is designed to be durable. The smaller feed tubes ensure safety for kids. But the downside is that you end up cutting and chopping produce into smaller bits to be fed through the tube.

There is a way to get more juice out of greens even with a centrifugal appliance. Tightly wrap the leaves in a cylindrical roll, either around a piece of carrot or ginger, or on its own and feed it through the feed tube.

This helps keep the leaves in contact with the blades longer and so it is able to extract more liquid.

You can feed full carrots and other vegetables too. This means that you don't spend all your free time cutting and chopping produce to feed through the gadget.

What is a cold press juicing machine? What is a fast juicing machine? What is a masticating juicing machine? Confused and clueless? Don't worry. We will answer all these and more in this short primer on juicing.

Unless you have been living under a rock, you would know by now that juicing is a health trend that has been going places with advanced juicing machines and technologies to help extract maximum juice from fruits and vegetables. Literally, they convert your fresh produce to liquid form with the skin, pulp and fiber being crushed and squeezed to extract every bit of goodness out of them.

If you plan on drinking fresh juice without any processing for nutritional benefits go for a cold press slow juicing machine as it preserves and extracts maximum nutrition from the juice.

In centrifugal juicing machines the rapid spinning of the disc causes heating of juice and the oxidation due to the air entering the juice due to the turbulence generated. The cold press slow juicing machines on the other hand rotate very slowly with hardly any agitation of juice.

Due to these factors juice extracted by this process has maximum minerals, vitamins and antioxidants which means your body gets the best possible nutrition from every glass.

Simple Tips for Mindful Eating

In conversations about healthy eating, dairy products sometimes unfairly get a bad rap. But dairy actually has essential nutrients that can be incorporated into a well-rounded daily diet.

indful eating doesn't have to be restrictive and you don't have to give up your favorite foods.

"Simply incorporating more foods that are crafted with integrity and align with your values into your day-to-day eating can go a long way toward helping you feel your best," says Kara Lydon, a registered dietitian nutritionist. As an intuitive eating counselor, Lydon advises people to stop looking at food as "good" or "bad" and instead, listen to their bodies and eat what feels best in the moment.

With those principles in mind, here are a few simple choices you can make to nourish your body and enjoy your food.

Snack Smart

Snacking can keep you satiated between meals and help you regulate your blood sugar and energy levels.

The next time you visit the dairy aisle, take a closer look at the labels and search for the term "grass-fed."

It can also be an opportunity to take in essential vitamins and nutrients. Common processed snack foods are often loaded with sodium, added sugars and trans fats. Try these wholesome alternatives: Greek yogurt with raw honey, hummus with carrot and celery sticks, apple slices with peanut butter, edamame, egg and cheese bites, nuts or fruit salad.

Choose Grass-Fed Dairy

In conversations about healthy eating, dairy products sometimes unfairly get a bad rap. But dairy actually has essential nutrients that can be incorporated into a well-rounded daily diet. Lydon says that it's helpful to be intentional with your choices. The next time you visit the dairy aisle, take a closer look at the labels and search for the term "grass-fed."

"Grass-fed cows produce dairy with significantly higher concentrations of beta-carotene and certain fatty acids, including conjugated linoleic acids and a more optimal omega-3/omega-6 ratio," says Lydon. "These nutrients play key roles in disease prevention, mood regulation, cognitive function and more."

Grass-fed dairy not only tastes better and is healthier for you versus grain-fed dairy, it's often more humanely produced. Check out brands committed to farming practices that are good for people, animals and the planet, like Truly Grass Fed. The premium brand of Irish dairy products makes cheese and butter that is always non-GMO, growth hormone rBST-free, and antibiotic free. Its cows live their best lives outside grazing on green grass maintained using regenerative farming practices. To learn more and find wholesome recipes, visit trulygrassfed.com.

Grow at Home

If you have the space, consider starting a small garden in your yard or even indoors on your kitchen counter. Growing your own food is sustainable and can help you connect more deeply to what you feed your family. What's more, being able to harvest produce at its peak means more nutritional value and flavor per bite. If you're feeling overwhelmed by the prospect of growing plants from seeds, start by buying a few pots of herbs, such as basil, chives and mint. These can be found at many a stores. They're relatively easy to maintain, and can instantly add zest to salads, soups and other meals.

Better eating should never feel like a sacrifice or leave you feeling hungry. The good news is that wholesome, healthier-for-you choices that nourish the body and soul abound today.

(StatePoint)

Honey for Athletes

BY
SRIDEVI
BALAMURUGAN

Honey was deliberately adulterated with high-fructose corn syrup (HFCS) at levels of 10%, 20%, 30%, 40%, and 50% (w/w). Sugar composition as a fingerprint was determined by HPLC for all samples. The following compositional properties were determined for pure and adulterated honey: moisture, total soluble solids, nitrogen, apparent viscosity, hydroxymethylfurfural (HMF), ash, sodium, calcium, potassium, proline, refractive index and diastatic activity." - Quoted by scienceDirect Journal:

Jonathan Horton, a member of the 2012 U.S. Olympic gymnastic team, faced a particular challenge during his training. He suffers from a problem with his blood sugars, which causes him to become shaky during workouts. His solution: honey. According to Horton, whenever he would feel weak and shaky from low blood sugar, he would take honey to boost his blood sugar. Kerry Walsh Jennings, a gold medalist in indoor and beach volleyball, swears by honey. Her diet includes almond butter and honey sandwiches. She eats them especially before competitions to give her energy.[courtesy: Coxhoney]

During the past 50 years, a significant volume of scientific research has consistently shown the critical role of glycogen for optimalathletic performance. Glycogen is how the body stores carbohydrates for energy at the muscular level.

Research indicates a correlation between training and competing with high muscle glycogen content and improved exertion capacity and overall performance.

Glycogen is the body's predominant source of energy during moderate- to high-intensity exertion

Results suggest that muscle glycogen availability can

During the past 50 years, a significant volume of scientific research has consistently shown the critical role of glycogen for optimal athletic performance. Glycogen is how the body stores carbohydrates for energy at the muscular level.

affect performance during both short-term and more prolonged high-intensity intermittent exercise1

(Courtesy: muscleround)

Richard Kreider, Professor and Department Head, Health and Kinesiology at Texas A&M University, conducted three studies that showed how honey can improve endurance exercise capacity.

All studies demonstrated that honey could be an alternative, improved option for endurance athletes and strength athletes, for improving athletic performance.

In "Honey and Sports nutrition: Report for the American Honey Board", 2001, Kreider highlights that it is important for athletes to maintain a consistent blood-sugar level throughout their exercise and competition. It is known that a high-glycemic index can cause spikes in blood sugar and energy. Honey has a moderate glycemic index (he measured it as 43 out of 100, where he placed white bread).

Resources:

[1] Balsom PD, Gaitanos GC, Soderlund K, Ekblom B. "High-intensity exercise and muscle glycogen availability in humans." Acta Physiol Scand. 1999 Apr;165(4):337-45.

[2] Boost athletic performance with honey. (2001, September 25). Retrieved August 09, 2016, from nutraingredients USA

[3] They Eat What? Food Secrets of Olympic Athletes. (2012, July 30). Retrieved August 09, 2016, from abcnews

HoneyBasket sells raw organic honey online, 100% lab tested, un-adulterated, with free shipping and money back guaranteed.

Flip Your Sandwich Game
Upside Down

Sandwiches reign supreme as one of America's favorite meals -- 47% of Americans eat a sandwich daily, according to a survey conducted by French's.

 andwiches reign supreme as one of America's favorite meals -- 47% of Americans eat a sandwich daily, according to a survey conducted by French's.

However, the same survey finds that consumers' number one pain point on sandwiches is overpowering or unbalanced flavor. If you're among the approximately one-third of people who don't currently add condiments to your sammies, a new lineup of creamier-than-ever spreads from French's may provide the balance you're seeking. Among the new condiments is French's Creamy Yellow Mustard Spread. Pairing well with meat and cheese for a better tasting sandwich, it has the tang of yellow mustard with a smoother finish and a thicker, creamier consistency.

Try the Creamy Yellow Mustard Spread in this Classic Turkey and Swiss recipe, which features hearty sandwich bread piled high with sliced deli turkey, avocado, Swiss cheese and veggies.

The new line-up of creamier mustards also includes Sweet Applewood and Honey Chipotle, all of which can be used as condiments, whisked into dressings, added to deviled eggs, or stirred into potato, tuna, shrimp or egg salads.

Try the Creamy Yellow Mustard Spread in this Classic Turkey and Swiss recipe, which features hearty sandwich bread piled high with

sliced deli turkey, avocado, Swiss cheese and veggies:

Ingredients: (4 Servings)

• 2 tablespoons French's Creamy Yellow Mustard Spread

• 4 slices multigrain sandwich bread

• 8 slices (about 8 ounces) deli-style turkey breast

• 4 slices Swiss cheese

• 1/2 medium avocado, peeled, pitted and sliced

• 1 medium vine-ripe tomato, sliced

• 1/4 cup red onion, cut into thin rings

• 4 leaves green leaf lettuce

Instructions:

1. Spread mustard on one side of each slice of bread.

2. Divide turkey between two slices of bread. Layer each with two slices of cheese. Top with avocado, tomato, red onion and lettuce. Top

with remaining bread slices. Secure sandwiches with toothpicks. Cut in half diagonally.

For more recipes and information, visit mccormick.com/frenchs.

If you're looking to add some balance to your sammies poolside, hosting, tailgating, picnicking or just everyday lunching, these new creamy mustard spreads can help put a delicious spin on the classics.

(Mccormick)

The Secret Ingredient

BY
TONY A
GRAYSON

There are chefs and meal preparers who seem to be willing to part with the ways and means to craft a coveted dish, but they don't tell you that they purposely left out or misrepresented a detail.

Commonly, both renowned chefs, and anyone who possesses the skills to cook, will not accurately part with the complete list of ingredients and/or the method to replicate a recipe for a popular food dish. The reasons for that are many. The acclaimed dish may be a centerpiece on the restaurant menu. The preparer believes that he or she may write a recipe book, and that particular dish might justify value in the book. Perhaps the recipe is a family recipe, handed down from an ancestor (Aunt Lucy).

"Who am I to give away Aunt Lucy's gift to our family?"

But, there are chefs and meal preparers who seem to be willing to part with the ways and means to craft a coveted dish, but they don't tell you that they purposely left out or misrepresented a detail. A novice culinary saboteur might muck around with the cooking temperature, but what purpose would there be in ruining the entire dish for an admirer of your cooking? No. Better it is for the vain to omit a single supporting ingredient (a secret ingredient).

"It looks like your dish, but it doesn't taste the same," said your admirer. You suggest that there was a lot of humidity that day. "Perhaps the extra juice of atmospheric moisture dampened your talent as you baked Aunt Lucy's masterpiece." You don't dare suggest, "Go ask your Grandma to teach you how to cook!" After all, your admirer suffers by your fault.

Try this recipe: "Roasted Squash, Tamarind Chile Glaze and Crisped Quinoa." Find the recipe online with that exact search. Suppose that you left out the annatto or the Thai Chile. Would the chef who originated the recipe approve? If you like to keep secrets, pray to God in secret. Web search Matthew 6: 5-8.

You just read a quote from Jesus Christ, written by his disciple, Matthew, who heard him say it. Prayer is your private conversation with God. Web search "The Lord's Prayer," which Jesus taught his disciples when they asked him how to pray to God. Think on how God perceives you when you pray to him in secret.

Suppose that your child comes to you crying for something that he or she wants. How do you react? Remember another time, when your child ran to you, hugged you, then looked up into your eyes and said, "I love you!" Consider beginning your secret prayer to God this way, "Father, thank you for your grace in my life."

Resource Box: In the name of Jesus Christ, pray to Father God. Ask him for his grace. Web search what you want to know about God, Jesus, the Holy Spirit, and other subjects in the Christian Bible at the online Bible Gateway, https://www.google.com/search?client=firefox-b-1-d&q=The+bible+gateway Through his grace, you will find hope.

Discover the benefits of being featured on a magazine

The pace of technological change sweeping boldly across business and society is breathtaking—and it is taking us from the digital age towards a new reality called post-digital era where everything is likely to change in the next ten years. It's no secret that the digital age has become increasingly integrated into our daily routine.

While technology continues to develop and become more intertwined with our everyday lives, people continue to remain tactile. People love to physically hold or touch something. As a matter of fact, the Nielson survey shows a decline for the second year in a row of eBook sales and an increase in print sales in the UK.

Our magazines have been released in print, electronic and flip in addition to web page and social media accounts. Here are the benefits to be feautred in our magazines:

INSPIRED READERS

A magazine provides a wealth of information, inspiration and creative ideas for readers. The information given to the reader may drive them to go out and visit stores/businesses and search online to find out more.

CREDIBILITY

Not just our magazine, many more magazines content is more likely be trusted by the reader as they have picked out the magazine for themselves. A survey conducted by Marketing Sherpa revealed 82% of participants trusted magazines when

"If you be featured on one of our magazines your name, brand and services will be shown around 40.000 networks, platforms and online stores like Amazon, Barnes & Noble, Rakuten, Blackwells, Waterstone's and so on over 190 countries. So you're everywhere. For instance, simply go to amazon and type Tosca Lee. You'll see her titles along with The Reader's House Magazine that she is fearured on the cover. "

making a purchase decision.

If you be featured on one of our magazines your name, brand and services will be shown around 40.000 networks, platforms and online stores like Amazon, Barnes & Noble, Rakuten, Blackwells, Waterstone's and so on over 190 countries. So you're everywhere. For instance, simply go to amazon and type Tosca Lee. You'll see her titles along with The Reader's House Magazine that she is fearured on the cover.

IT LASTS

We make the magazine available both print and electronic and make it available on the market forever. You can order or download whenever you want. . Commit to a long-term campaign of advertising/publicity and you can build your recognition over time.

BRAND POWER

Take the opportunity to create consistency across all your channels, so wherever people come into contact with you they will see the same messages and images.

Before we make our magazines available for distribution, we make sure all the information about you, your product/services, keywords and links inserted to the metadata form. Then you will reach new audiences and become a well-recognized brand both local and national business. Our magazines have a great reputation for interest and authority. People will trust what they see, and your brand will benefit as a result.

HIGH QUALITY

High quality images and pages are a must for our magazines. This allows for the best representation of you and your products/services.

READER'S CONFIDENCE

No fake news and cybercrime. Readers trust our magazines.

TARGETED AUDIENCE

If your business is local, then our local issues are the ideal way to connect directly to your potential customers. They are interested and involved in their local community, so they will be interested in you too. Because they are proud of where they live, readers will probably prefer to buy from local businesses.

(Newyox Media)

BENGAL TIGER
BAR & RESTAURANT

Bengal Tiger's food and drink has been acclaimed in all of London for its delicious taste and great quality.

Serving you the best INDIAN FOOD experience is what we love, it is what we do and it is what everyone at Bengal Tiger is passionate about. Which is why we are different than others.

"Tikka Makes You Holla!"

The Reader's House

 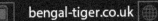

Available both print and electronic all over the globe.

Taste London reaches more then 40.000
retailers (including Amazon, Barnes & Noble
Waterstones, Blackwells, and local independent
bookstores in the United States.)

Visit thereadershouse.co.uk for more